We've Got to ~~Stop~~ *Start* Meeting & Emailing Like This!

20 PROVEN PRACTICES
TO SAVE TIME,
BOOST MORALE
& IMPROVE RESULTS

George Lowe & Tony Jeary

We've Got to ~~Stop~~ *Start* Meeting & Emailing Like This!

20 Proven Practices to Save Time, Boost Morale and Improve Results

Printed in the United States of America
ISBN: 978-0-9821246-1-1

Credits

Developmental & Contributing Editor	Juli Baldwin, The Baldwin Group, Dallas, TX info@BaldwinGrp.com
Copy Editor	Kathleen Green, Positively Proofed, Plano, TX info@positivelyproofed.com
Design, Art Direction, and Production	Melissa Cabana, Back Porch Creative, Plano, TX info@backporchcreative.com

Table of Contents

Outbound

Introduction

What if your organization could…

✓ Reduce time spent in meetings by 20 percent or more?

✓ Get back precious time wasted on inefficient handling of email?

✓ Increase productivity by implementing a strategic, clear, focused approach to meetings and emails?

✓ Cultivate a culture that encourages preparation, clear communications and rigorous follow-up?

Two of the most common factors preventing positive results in organizations are unproductive meetings and ineffective email communication. In fact, when people are asked to rate their organization's efficiency and effectiveness on a 1-to-10 scale in these two areas, their ratings are on average a 5 or lower. No wonder so many people dread attending meetings and dealing with their email!

Think about what that 5 rating costs you and your organization every day in terms of productivity, morale and results. What would happen if your organization could increase its score to an 8 or 9? It would change you and your entire organization.

Yet many leaders take meeting and email effectiveness for granted. In our experience, most organizations offer minimal to no training in these areas, assuming instead that people know how to effectively conduct meetings and use email. But given that these two routine activities alone consume 30 percent to 50 percent of your team members' time, are you willing to take that chance?

Most organizations could significantly improve their Return on Investment (ROI) and Return on Effort (ROE) for meeting and emailing if they knew what to change and crafted strategic communication standards. Improving meeting and email execution is primarily an awareness issue. That's why this little book can have such a dramatic impact.

ASK YOURSELF

✦ How many hours a week do you waste in inefficient meetings and on ineffective emails?

✦ How often are you in a meeting where you think your time would be better spent elsewhere?

✦ Do you consider meetings and emailing "necessary evils" or strategic tools?

✦ How much better would your work life be if these strategic tools were more refined for greater effectiveness?

Based on our work over the past 20 years with many of the world's largest corporations, we have identified 10 meeting best practices and 10 email best practices that can revolutionize your culture, dramatically increase your team's results, productivity and morale, and significantly improve your internal and external communications.

We've been training people on these practices for years and have seen the results that prove they work. Virtually everyone in your organization can **learn them in just a few hours and start seeing**

results immediately. They are easy to execute and to deploy across an entire team simultaneously. And because several of the concepts apply to both meetings and emails, learning and applying them is even easier.

Enhancing meeting and email effectiveness is so powerful and far-reaching that it often produces a radical transformation that creates and sustains **substantial results.** When used as a primer to change your organization's culture and habits around meetings and email, this book can **add 5 to 10 hours a week back into every person's schedule.** And in today's fast-paced world, that's like gold!

Implement the practices outlined in this book and begin enjoying improved morale, increased productivity and more positive RESULTS in your organization TODAY.

We've Got to ~~Stop~~ *Start* Meeting & Emailing Like This!

Part I: Meetings

Meetings have a huge impact on an organization's success – or its failure. That is why it is extremely important for leaders to invest time and energy in making them better. Consider these facts:

✦ Many of us will spend as much as one-half of our working life in meetings.

✦ At least one-third of all meetings are perceived by some attendees to be either unnecessary or unproductive.

✦ Virtually all meetings have some unproductive segments.

Time is at a premium today, and reducing the number and/or length of meetings represents a high-leverage timesaver. For most organizations, even minor improvements can save significant time considering the number of meetings involved and the number of people in attendance. And in a do-more-with-less world, meetings are a significant potential source of productivity improvements.

Meetings that produce results are designed to convey key information, find opportunities or solve problems, change or reinforce others' thinking and drive specific outcomes. Effective meeting management revolves around three key areas: preparation, delivery and follow-up. Well-executed meetings enable people to show up prepared, efficiently absorb the intended message, address issues at hand, and immediately get to work executing the right things.

In this section of the book, we will share meeting best practices that will help you:

✦ Make your meetings more powerful, inspiring and action-oriented;

✦ Save time in both preparation and actual meetings;

✦ Increase productivity through clarity and focus;

✦ Drive execution and create better results.

The ability to lead efficient and effective meetings can be a major contributor to your professional credibility, image and success. Implement the practices in this section, and you will build a reputation for not wasting others' time. You will also earn the respect of people who attend your meetings, and they will be more enthusiastic about attending the next one.

1. Set and Follow Written Meeting Standards

One of the best approaches we've found for improving meeting management across an organization is setting – *and following* – written standards for meetings. Meeting standards document agreed-upon best practices for how your organization will plan, facilitate and communicate with respect to meetings, as well as how team members should participate.

Once set, communicating the standards throughout the organization is critical. In our experience, standards are most effective when they cascade as a directive from top leadership. Perhaps unlike some organizational mandates, meeting standards are usually welcomed due to the positive impact on virtually everyone. Using reminders such as memory cards and posting the standards in conference rooms will further embed the standards within your culture. Be specific – not general – in your standards.

Even if you are not a senior leader, you can get this movement for better meetings started by setting meeting standards for your team or organizational unit. As others see the success you're having with your meetings, the standards will naturally spread throughout the organization.

When developing your standards, choose the 10 core practices that are best for your needs, your organization and your culture. What works at a high-tech firm may not work at a hospital, for example. The point is to set standards that are in sync with your existing culture and then incorporate them into the collective mindset. On the following page are our recommended meeting standards.

Meeting Standards

1. Have a clear purpose and defined objective(s) for every meeting.

2. Ensure that the right people are either in the room, on the phone or represented.

3. Create *and follow* a realistic, timed agenda.

4. Start and end meetings on time.

5. Acknowledge that achieving winning outcomes is not just the meeting leader's responsibility, but everyone's responsibility.

6. Facilitate for results so that everyone stays involved and engaged.

7. Take thorough notes, documenting important discussion points, outcomes and agreements.

8. Develop a "who does what by when" action plan.

9. Publish meeting notes and action plans quickly, and follow up to ensure timely execution.

10. Strategically cascade meeting outcomes promptly and consistently to others in the organization.

Set and communicate ground rules at the start of every meeting. Below are some ground rules you may want to adopt:
- ✦ Everyone participates.
- ✦ Take breaks only at scheduled times.
- ✦ Turn off cellular phones, laptops and tablets.
- ✦ Post interesting but off-agenda topics for discussion at the end of the session if time permits.

Preparation

2. Define Your Objectives

Skilled meeting leaders agree that proper preparation is one of the most important aspects of the meeting management process. Comprehensive planning should be the normal foundation for any meeting. But in today's busy world, what is typically viewed as optional preparation often gets set aside in favor of tasks considered to be more urgent. Yet **advanced planning is well worth your time because it significantly increases the likelihood that meetings can be shortened and made more effective,** thereby saving everyone time and the organization money. Leverage assistants or other team members to support when possible.

The very first step in planning any meeting is to define your objective(s). Without absolute clarity regarding what you want to accomplish through a meeting, you limit your chances of achieving the best possible results. If you want to hit the target, you have to know where you're aiming.

Identifying your objectives from the outset pays off in other ways, too. **People will be more engaged, collaborative and productive when they know *why* they are being brought into a meeting and *what* specifically they are expected to contribute.** If they don't clearly understand the purpose of a meeting, they won't be mentally prepared (at best); at worst, they may be no-shows. Even if you have the power to compel them to attend, they may physically be present at your meeting, but they likely will not be engaged in the process.

To gain true clarity of purpose, we recommend use of the "reporter's questions" to help you identify and define specific objectives:

What	What is my desired outcome? What exact actions do I want to happen as a result of this meeting?
Who	Who can help accomplish the desired outcome? Who needs to be in the loop?
When	When does this need to happen? Are there interim deadlines? What are the consequences of not meeting the timeframe?
Why	Why do we want this to happen? What's in it for me and for others? Will there be any objections? If yes, how do I overcome them?
How	Do we need to follow specific methods, or can we focus more on results than process? Is cost a factor?

Once you have identified the objectives, strategically choose the medium that will best support those objectives and help you achieve your desired results. You might discover that holding a group meeting is neither necessary nor the best method for accomplishing your objectives. Here are some distinctions to consider:

+ If immediate resolution is needed, use the phone or meet face-to-face with the key players needed to make a decision.

+ If several people are involved and/or interaction and collaboration are needed, use a meeting, conference call or video conference.

+ Emotional disagreements and personal conflicts are best handled with face-to-face contact or a phone call.

+ Company-wide statements and addresses by the CEO or other senior management should be cascaded throughout the organization through follow-up meetings conducted by lower-level leaders.

Preparation

3. Involve the Right People

Involving the wrong people is a chronic driver of ineffective, non-productive meetings. Conversely, you can **dramatically improve teamwork and results by getting the right people in the room for every meeting.**

Before sending meeting invitations, carefully consider who you need in order to get the job done. Our recommendation is that you write down your objective and then mentally tick through the following list while asking yourself, "Who do I need to achieve the objective?"

- ✦ **Information:** Who has the data or information needed to make a decision or develop a solution?

- ✦ **Function:** Which departments need to be represented and will carry out the actions determined?

- ✦ **Regional:** Are there unique cultural or geographic market considerations? Who can best represent these?

- ✦ **Level:** Who needs to know about this? Who has decision-making capability and authority on this issue?

- ✦ **Diversity:** Am I involving a broad enough array of viewpoints, disciplines, levels, etc.?

- ✦ **Inclusiveness:** Am I involving people from all sides of the issue?

Especially with complex, cross-functional matters, you may want to seek input from key stakeholders to determine who should be involved. For particularly critical or controversial issues, we recommend *Participant Mapping.* This technique determines, in advance of the meeting, who has the power on a particular issue and what their position going into the meeting might be. (A blank Participant Map is available in "Forms and Resources" at the end of this section.)

One of the most powerful ways to boost productivity throughout your organization is to understand that **not everyone needs to be in every meeting or attend a meeting for the full duration.** With careful agenda development and management, you can involve specific people at specific times for specific reasons, boosting everyone's productivity. Consider these options:

✦ Place those who will bring important information, data or reports – but aren't necessary for other parts of the meeting – early on the agenda and excuse them following their segment.

✦ People who are needed only for "next steps" can arrive for the recap. For example, a communications director responsible for cascading information throughout the organization probably doesn't need to attend the full meeting.

✦ If a key individual can't attend in person, perhaps they can join by phone or video conference. Another option is to get their "take" on the issues beforehand and be prepared to speak on their behalf, or ask them to send an empowered representative who has been briefed in advance.

✦ Senior leaders and/or decision makers can be invited to attend only the recap if they agree not to overturn decisions unless they are seriously off the mark. Or you can ask the applicable leader to approve, in advance, outcomes within certain boundaries. This allows the group to decide details, yet ensures the group's plan will be approved or funded.

✦ For maximum impact, you must get those people who attend only the recap segment up to speed quickly. Having the notetaker email the meeting notes thus far to these attendees 5 to 10 minutes before they are scheduled to arrive allows them to walk into the meeting ready to engage and participate.

Preparation

4. Create a Timed Agenda

A timed agenda is the foundation of a successful meeting. You will achieve better results when people know specifically what tasks and timing to expect. Having a timed agenda helps the meeting leader stay on track and keep the group moving forward. It also allows participants to arrive when they are needed and depart when their segment is complete.

Whenever possible, develop the agenda well in advance of the meeting and distribute it with the meeting notice. It is essential, however, that one be agreed to before the meeting begins. If an agenda has not been prepared and distributed ahead of time, build it "live" onscreen or on a whiteboard at the outset of the meeting.

An effective meeting agenda establishes the order of different segments, specifies the *what, why, how* and *who* for each segment and allocates time for each segment. A sample timed agenda is shown on the next page and a blank form is available in "Forms and Resources" at the end of this section. Note the use of action words in the "what" column. Possibilities include *alert, transfer, communicate, educate, discuss, agree, drive, design, schedule, resolve, assign* and *decide.*

To create your agenda, we recommend using the 3-D Outline™ Builder software (www.TonyJeary.com), which automates and accelerates many aspects of agenda development and allows the meeting organizer to think through the steps needed to achieve the meeting objectives. A blank 3-D Outline can be found in "Forms and Resources" at the end of this section.

Presentation Title: Sale & Marketing Strategy Meeting
Audience: 6 executives and decision-makers
at prospect location (name company)

Delivery Date: 10-01-2013
Start Time: 9:00 am
End Time: 10:00 am

Objectives:
+ Convey potential of product value to prospective client
+ Educate on our background to credentialize
+ Help prepare them to overcome objections
+ Gain buy-in

Final Preparation: ❑ Hard copy tools/templates   ❑
                   ❑ Copy of Executive Summary for all   ❑

#	TIME	WHAT	WHY	HOW	WHO
1	2	Host Introduction	Introduce and credentialize us to group	Use pre-written bio card along with ad lib of how met	Main contact
2	2	Purpose (Objectives) Process (Agenda) Payoff (What's in It for Them)	Gain audience involvement and set expectations	Slides, present	Tony
3	2	Why you?	Share the reasons we want to collaborate and show we've done homework on them	Slides, present	George
4	2	Brief History	Share foundation of who we are	Share story, present	Tony
5	13	Why us? Why now? - Common questions - Importance and value of content - Compress time	Share benefits of working together	Slides, present; show statistics, share successes	Tony
6	9	How will this drive sales? - Methodology - Tools	Show depth of offering	Slides, demonstrate how to utilize tools (have hard copy available)	George
7	8	How do you get buy-in for change? - Common objections and how to overcome	Arm them with information to overcome potential objections for buy-in	Discussion, build Objections Matrix live	Tony
8	15	General Discussion and Q&A - General Q&A - Show additional tools based on questions	Allow them to be heard; listen to issues	Discussion, live note-taking on issues; demonstrate additional tools if applicable	George
9	7	Gain Buy-in and Close	Recap meeting, close gaps, and get buy-in	Discussion, exercise with take-aways, pass out Executive Summary, close	Tony
	60 min.				

Preparation

5. Manage the Details

Once you have determined the purpose of the meeting, identified who can help achieve your objective(s) and created an agenda, you're ready for the final step of meeting preparation: handling the details. You might think that simple activities such as scheduling the meeting, sending out invitations and organizing the meeting room wouldn't warrant mentioning, but we often find it's these very details that trip up many meeting leaders.

You can be diligent in following the first three preparation practices (determining objective, people and agenda), but if you learn the day before the meeting that half the sales team can't attend or you discover at the last minute that an AV component is missing, your meeting likely won't be as effective or efficient as you had hoped. Managing the small things can pay big dividends. Here are key meeting details that merit advanced planning. In addition, a comprehensive planning checklist is available in "Forms and Resources."

Schedule the Meeting

The saying, "Timing is everything" takes on special significance in the context of meetings. Of course, it's best to schedule meetings as far in advance as possible. In addition, stay away from communication Dead Zones and leverage Opportunity Zones.

Dead Zones are those times when certain topics or requests should be avoided. For example:

✦ Very late in the day, especially on Fridays, and right before holiday breaks;

✦ During unique departmental constraints that dictate when people are unusually busy (such as the accounting department during year-end close, the sales team leading up to a trade show, or manufacturing during a new product launch).

Opportunity Zones represent communication "sweet spots," or the best times to address certain matters. For example:

✦ When the landscape is ideal (e.g., ask for project funding after quarterly profits are announced and before budgets are locked down for the next year);

✦ When potential interruptions are minimized;

✦ Using travel time for one-on-one meetings and relationship building.

Send a Meeting Notice

Meeting invitations are an important element of meeting success. Clarity at the invitation stage sets a better mindset for results during the meeting itself. Effective meeting invitations:

✦ Share the purpose or objectives of the meeting;

✦ Include the agenda and pre-reading or pre-work files;

✦ Communicate what each person is expected to bring to the meeting or provide in advance.

Leverage calendaring systems (e.g., Microsoft Outlook) to invite attendees and track RSVPs. Make contact with key people to assure they'll either attend or be represented.

Get Organized

A little bit of time invested in pre-meeting preparation ensures your meeting will run more smoothly. Some items to consider:

✦ In advance of the meeting:
  ✧ Schedule the meeting room or location;
  ✧ Gather data, reference materials, etc.;
  ✧ Produce agendas and handouts on computer or paper.

✦ Day of the meeting:
  ✧ Take computer and/or computer files with presentations;
  ✧ Confirm or customize room arrangement;
  ✧ Check equipment placement (screen, projector, computers, microphones);
  ✧ Locate supplies (pointer, markers, masking tape, etc.);
  ✧ Perform a technical rehearsal (computers, projectors, sound levels, lighting, etc.).

Preparation → Delivery

6. Facilitate for Results

Many leaders don't realize the benefits of effective meeting facilitation. How well you facilitate can often make or break a meeting and significantly impact results. **Facilitation actually begins at the preparation stage, continues throughout the meeting and extends beyond the meeting into the follow-up stage.** Keeping people engaged and involved from beginning to end is vital to ensuring that meeting objectives are achieved and translated into action.

Following are facilitation best practices. In addition, you will find more Facilitation Tips in "Forms and Resources."

✦ **Plan to facilitate.** When preparing the agenda, consciously plan how much time you will spend presenting versus facilitating. If you're planning to spend the majority of your time presenting, consider a shift to focus more on leading the group toward a solution or the accomplishment of your objective.

✦ **Facilitate for "wins."** A secret to keeping people engaged during a meeting is to facilitate for a win/win. The goal of the meeting is to accomplish your objective(s); if you can do it in such a way that participants feel valued, that's the icing on the cake. When people share thoughts or ideas that support your objective(s), draw them out by saying, "Tell me more about that." As they share their insights and expertise, not only will they think they are making a genuine contribution, but they can also create *Peer Trust Transference* in which your message as the meeting leader is reinforced and validated.

✦ **Recap through *Verbal Surveying.*** At various points in the meeting, pause to solicit feedback, summarize progress and verify the direction you're headed. For example: "At the beginning of the meeting, we said we would do…. We are now halfway through, and this is what we've covered…. Here is what we have left to do…. How do you think it's going? Do we need to speed up or slow down?" Based on input from participants, make adjustments as necessary and move forward. In lengthy meetings or sessions with multiple defined objectives, recap at the end of each topic and then again at the end of the meeting.

✦ **Be real, not perfect.** Your job at the front of the room is not to have every answer or to prove how smart you are, but rather to be credible, effective and, most importantly, real. People who can relate to you as a human being will be more likely to help you achieve your goals. Know the difference between being right and being effective. Being right doesn't ensure you'll achieve your objectives. It's a rare meeting leader who doesn't make some type of mistake during a session. Don't be afraid to laugh at yourself when you make a mistake; it's humanizing and helps you connect with the group. (Note: There are, of course, exceptions when perfect accuracy does matter.)

✦ **Work the agenda and limit off-agenda discussions.** It's your job to ensure the meeting stays on track so that the results promised by the agenda are actually delivered. Use *HUHY (Help Us Help You)* Cards – index cards on which meeting participants document off-agenda questions to be addressed at a later time. Of course, it's okay under certain circumstances to depart from the planned agenda if necessary to accomplish the stated objectives, for example, if new data becomes available that materially changes the situation.

✦ Always be respectful, civil and sensitive when engaging others to help you accomplish your objectives. Even if you're the boss and have the power to demand support, it's much more effective to courteously ask for what you want. People want respect; give it to them.

Preparation → Delivery

7. Take Clear and Concise Notes

Unless your agenda has only one item and the only possible outcomes are "yes" or "no," you need good meeting notes. It does little good to have a clear objective and the right people gathered to address that objective if no one captures what is discussed and which actions are agreed upon.

When information is written down, clarity moves to the highest level. Effective meeting notes include:

✦ Who attended;

✦ Topics discussed;

✦ Key outcomes and agreements;

✦ Actions agreed to.

At the beginning of the meeting, assign a scribe to capture notes. If you have the resources, bringing in a dedicated scribe who is not a meeting participant often enables the group to work through the agenda more quickly. (Outside scribes do not need to be experts in the subject matter of the meeting, but they do need to understand the jargon and acronyms typically used by the group.)

There are three levels of note taking:

1. Good – handwritten on a whiteboard or flip chart.

2. Better – typed on a computer.

3. **Best – live capture using two sets of a projector and a screen**, one set for delivering presentations and meeting content, and the other set for simultaneously capturing meeting notes and

action plans. If a two-screen set-up is not practical, the scribe can switch back and forth between a "notes page" and the presentations material.

Live capture of meeting notes is both highly efficient and very effective. Because the notes are typed during the meeting, they are available to be sent immediately after. In addition, seeing the notes live onscreen as they are taken ensures clarity and allows for on-the-spot corrections or revisions. And finally, when people see their words in writing, they are more likely to own the actions and outcomes. It facilitates agreement and ensures each participant is on the same page.

Meeting notes and action plans should be published and sent within hours. Quickly edit the notes for tone, tact and clarity to create an easy-to-understand document. (This is especially important for those who did not attend the meeting.) However, keep in mind the concept of *Production Before Perfection (PBP)* – it's better to send good notes within an hour than perfect notes days later.

When publishing meeting notes, place the action-planning content (who will do what by when) near the top of the document so that it remains top of mind for recipients. Documents and presentations used in the meeting can be included as attachments. Meeting notes are also a good place to recognize accomplishments and "wins," and to thank those who made significant contributions to the outcomes.

Preparation → Delivery

8. Conquer Conference Calls and Virtual Meetings

The basics of meeting management for audio conference calls, video and web conferencing, and mixed live/electronic meetings are the same as for comparable face-to-face meetings. In virtual meetings, however, maintaining engagement among participants can be challenging, especially since people often multitask. This difference in meeting dynamics (no camaraderie among participants) and the lack of visual feedback (e.g., body language and facial expressions) mean that good facilitation is even more critical.

✦ **Invite participants to email or text their questions.** Arrange for someone to sit next to you to review and qualify the questions as they come in while you continue the meeting.

✦ **Use multiple presenters and/or facilitators.** This not only provides a change of pace that keeps people interested, but also creates *breathing space* for you, the meeting leader. It is best to plan this in advance when possible and even have a short rehearsal when possible to designate specific topics for each person's input.

✦ **Check in with participants frequently.** Using *Verbal Surveying* to periodically recap progress is even more important in virtual meetings to ensure everyone is in agreement and on the same page.

✦ **Use *Targeted Polling* to keep people engaged.** Whereas *Verbal Surveying* involves asking the group for feedback or comment, *Targeted Polling* is directed at one person (e.g., "Jane, what do you think about what John just said?"). Asking specific people specific questions keeps them tuned in because they never know if you might call on them next.

Here are some additional tips to make your conference calls and virtual meetings more effective:

Pre-Meeting

✦ Provide the agenda and material to be presented. Combine all documents in one PDF file, with pages numbered.

✦ Arrive at least 10 minutes before the scheduled start time and familiarize yourself with the audio and/or video system.

Opening

✦ Introduce participants, set expectations and remind everyone to mute their phones unless speaking.

✦ Review the agenda and confirm that all participants have their document packages onscreen.

Delivery

✦ Identify each stage of the agenda and indicate by page number which document the group should be looking at.

✦ Pause frequently to allow people to join the conversation.

✦ As agreements are reached and topics are about to be closed, do a "roll call" question such as, "Does anyone have anything else on this...Sally, Chris, Pat, Pete, Fred...?"

✦ Clear meeting notes and action plans are essential, so using a designated scribe is recommended.

Follow-up

✦ Follow up with notes via email and individual phone calls if necessary to add clarity to outcomes and action plans.

Preparation → Delivery → **Follow-up**

9. Develop a Clear Action Plan and Then Follow Up

The goal of any meeting is to accomplish the defined objective. Frequently, that requires people to take independent action after the meeting is over. Although action planning starts during the meeting, it is the foundation for all activity and the results that occur *after* the meeting.

If you want to **drive exceptional results, action planning is perhaps the most important part of the meeting.** As such, it deserves its own segment on the agenda. When you build the timed agenda, make certain you leave plenty of time at the end for action planning. During the meeting, watch the clock and stay on track. Don't make the mistake of spending so much time sharing data, discussing options and hearing opinions that you short-change the action-planning segment.

Action planning is essentially deciding "who will do what when." A major cause of lost productivity is a lack of *Action Clarity*, wherein a meeting occurs and agreements are made, but few or none are clear on exactly what is to happen next and who is responsible. *Action Clarity* **occurs when agreements are translated into an action plan** – a list of clearly defined next steps. This process is simple and very effective, yet often overlooked.

Action planning can be done in a variety of ways, but the end result is more or less the same. Action planning should include, at a minimum:

✦ Determining next steps (what);

✦ Setting assignments (who);

✦ Deciding timing for next steps (when).

Once the action plan is agreed on, it must be clearly documented in the meeting notes. Live note-taking is critical during action planning because it allows everyone to see in writing what they are agreeing to do and how their piece fits into the overall plan. When the plan is completed, go around the room and check in with people by name to confirm their action(s) and timeline(s).

Follow-up is essential in order to translate the action plan into concrete actions and drive results. Simply publishing the meeting notes and action plan usually isn't enough to ensure action. As deadlines approach, follow up with people to assess progress. If there are concerns or issues that could potentially derail progress, offer to help find support to get the work back on track. Be sure to recognize and thank those who are on track to deliver.

As you follow up, document the status of each action item on your action plan and add comments as necessary. Send updates to the group and other stakeholders to keep everyone apprised of progress. Below is a simple action plan and follow-up report. A blank form is available in "Forms and Resources" at the end of this section.

Action Plan & Follow-up Report			
WHAT	**WHO**	**BY WHEN**	**STATUS/COMMENTS**
Marketing "Concept B" – develop budget details & launch plans	Chris	Friday 22nd	
Verbally brief selected senior execs on rationale for selection of "Concept B" & publish meeting notes	Pat	Today	Notes published; CEO out until next week
Schedule "Concept B" kickoff meeting for sales team & publish meeting notice	David	Friday 29th	
Schedule final approval meeting for this group early in week of the 23rd	Pat	Tomorrow	

Preparation → Delivery → **Follow-up**

10. Cascade Outcomes to Others

While most people are familiar with the concept of cascading, many don't think of it with respect to meetings. Yet **cascading meeting outcomes and action plans is essential for achieving results.** The impact of meeting outcomes usually extends far beyond the people sitting in the room (or on the call). Consequently, that information must be communicated to the people who are affected but were not present in the meeting. Those people might be just down the hall, or they might be in other departments, at other levels of the organization or in different parts of the world.

Cascading outcomes applies to nearly all meetings, whether face-to-face or virtual, large or small, internal or external. Sales presentations are a prime external example. At Tony Jeary International, we often have sales meetings with key contacts who then have to cascade the information we presented with others in the organization, such as the C-suite, human resources or training and development department.

There are two significant obstacles to cascading outcomes and action plans. The first is timely execution. Attendees frequently leave meetings with assigned action items and corresponding deadlines. Cascading information to other people often becomes just another item on an already lengthy to-do list. Without intentional effort, communicating outcomes can easily fall by the wayside.

The second challenge is message consistency and clarity. As information is cascaded, it tends to get changed or diluted, just as in the childhood "telephone game" where a message whispered from one person to another is often very different at the end of the line than it was at the beginning. In order to effectively execute action plans and drive results, the message received by those in the meeting has to be the same message received by team members two and three levels down.

Here are three best practices that will **ensure meeting outcomes are cascaded both quickly and consistently:**

1. **Strategically think about cascading during the preparation stage.** Most people don't think about cascading information until the end of, or after, a meeting (if at all). You will achieve better results if you consider cascading as you plan your meeting:

   ✦ What information, agreements and outcomes will need to be shared? Which action items need to be delegated?

   ✦ Whom will these items need to be shared with?

   ✦ Who will be responsible for cascading this information?

   ✦ How can this information best be communicated?

2. **Create and distribute a cascading tool.** One of the most powerful ways to ensure timely and consistent communication of outcomes is to utilize a tool – such as a handout, presentation, video or email – that covers key information. Providing meeting attendees with a cascading tool ensures the message is consistent no matter how many times it is repeated or who is doing the communicating. Without such a tool, people will naturally tend to put their "spin" on your message. A cascading tool also speeds up execution. When most of the communication work has been done for them, attendees can easily and quickly pass information on to others. Selective redistribution of meeting notes, along with relevant materials (data, presentations, etc.), is the easiest way to cascade outcomes. In some cases, however, a more formal process (such as a series of meetings) may be appropriate.

3. **Set expectations and gain agreement.** At the beginning of the meeting, be sure to set the expectation that outcomes and action plans will need to be cascaded. People tend to be more engaged in a meeting when they know they will be responsible for sharing the message with others. At the end of the meeting, agree to a timetable for when and how information will be cascaded.

Meeting VIPs
(Very Important Points)

1. Set and follow written standards. Meeting standards document core best practices for how your organization will plan, facilitate and communicate with respect to meetings.

PREPARATION

2. Define your objectives. People are more engaged, collaborative and productive when they know *why* they are being brought into a meeting and *what* specifically they are expected to contribute.

3. Involve the right people. Consider what data you need, which departments and decision makers should be present and whether you have a variety of viewpoints. Boost productivity by involving specific people at specific times for specific reasons. Leverage calendaring systems.

4. Create a timed agenda in advance. An effective meeting agenda specifies the *what, why, how, who* and *how* long for each segment.

5. Manage the details. Schedule meetings as far in advance as possible, staying away from communication Dead Zones and leveraging Opportunity Zones. Include the objective, agenda and any pre-reading files in meeting notices. Arrive early on meeting day to get organized.

DELIVERY

6. Facilitate for results. Keep people engaged from start to finish by facilitating for wins – achieving your objective *and* valuing their contributions. Use *Verbal Surveying* to recap at key points in the meeting.

7. **Take clear and concise notes.** Capture notes live onscreen during the meeting and publish within hours. Effective notes include who attended, topics discussed, key outcomes and agreements, and action plans.

8. **Conquer conference calls and virtual meetings.** Differences in meeting dynamics mean that good facilitation is even more critical. Use multiple presenters, *Verbal Surveying* and *Targeted Polling* to keep participants engaged and focused. Provide a simple PDF with numbered pages.

FOLLOW-UP

9. **Develop a clear action plan and then follow up.** Action planning is so critical that it must have a designated spot on the agenda. Action clarity occurs when agreements are translated into a written action plan – a list of who will do what when. Following up with each person on the plan is essential in order to translate the plan into concrete actions and to drive results.

10. **Cascade outcomes to others.** Ensure that meeting outcomes and action plans are cascaded both quickly and consistently by preparing in advance, setting expectations during the meeting, and creating and utilizing a cascading tool.

Forms & Resources

All Forms and Resources are available for download at www.TonyJeary.com.

Participant Map

Participant Map				
ISSUE:				
OBJECTIVE:				
INDIVIDUAL'S NAME	**POWER TO INFLUENCE**	**STRENGTH OF POSITION**	**NOTES**	**INVITE?**
	1 2 3	1 2 3		
	1 2 3	1 2 3		
	1 2 3	1 2 3		
	1 2 3	1 2 3		
	1 2 3	1 2 3		

Note: 1 designates the lowest power/strength; 3 the highest.

Important Note: Because they tend to use brief (and perhaps blunt) statements about issues and positions that are based largely on opinions, Participant Maps should be treated as very sensitive documents. Generally, they are intended for the personal and private use of the meeting leader and should not be circulated.

Presentation Title: **Delivery Date:**

Audience: **Start Time:**

End Time:

Objectives:

✦   ✦

✦   ✦

Final Preparation: ❑   ❑

                  ❑ | ❑

#	TIME	WHAT	WHY	HOW	WHO
1					
2					
3					
4					
5					
6					
7					
8					
	min.				

Meeting Checklist

Meeting Notice

❑ Include agenda and pre-reading or pre-work files

❑ Track RSVPs

Take to Meeting

❑ Meeting files, including data, reference materials, etc.

❑ Computer/computer files with presentations

❑ Participant agendas on computer or paper

❑ Handouts or physical properties

On-Site Setup

❑ Facility host liaison

❑ Catering arrangements

❑ Directional signs

❑ Location of restrooms

❑ Heating/AC controls

Room Arrangements

❑ Confirm/"make it your own"

❑ Equipment placement (screen, projector, computers, microphones)

❑ Supplies (pointer, markers, masking tape, etc.)

❑ Materials placement (handouts, name tags, place cards)

❑ Technical rehearsal:
  ✦ Computers and other equipment functioning
  ✦ Lighting and sound control levels set
  ✦ Confirm sightlines/slide legibility

Last 10 to 30 Minutes

❑ Personal prep and focus

❑ Freshen up attire

❑ Body language check

❑ Connect with host and confirm host introduction

❑ Greet participants as they arrive

Facilitation Tips

At the opening:

- ✦ Arrive early to meet and greet, paying special attention to critical participants and VIPs.
- ✦ Start and end on time.
- ✦ Introduce attendees, encourage all to participate and declare that all points of view are welcome.
- ✦ Set expectations and ground rules that fit your culture (e.g., lids down on laptops, phones off).
- ✦ Assign or confirm roles, such as topic leaders/facilitators, scribe and timekeeper.

Throughout the meeting

- ✦ Be courteous and professional, remembering "please" and "thank you."
- ✦ Build in variety through Q&A, *Business Entertainment* and the use of different facilitators for varied segments.
- ✦ Manage the energy and attitude in the room by modeling what you want.
- ✦ Use general questions to solicit comments and do a roll call to garner responses from specific people.
- ✦ Defer any emotional disagreements to an "offline" forum.

At the recap

- ✦ Summarize agreements and decisions.
- ✦ Survey participants and make adjustments as necessary.
- ✦ Recognize people who made unique contributions (e.g., triggering the "aha" moment).

At the close

- ✦ Review session notes, addressing any unclear items.
- ✦ Review action plan, paying attention to timelines.
- ✦ Discuss best takeaways.
- ✦ Thank all for their enthusiastic participation.

Action Planning & Follow-up Form

WHAT	WHO	BY WHEN	STATUS/COMMENTS

 **Part II:** **Emails**

Email is a powerful tool that has fundamentally changed the way we communicate in business. Utilized in conjunction with meetings, email becomes an even greater strategic asset. It is the perfect vehicle for distributing meeting notices, agendas and pre-reading materials, communicating action plans and cascading outcomes.

Yet as beneficial as it is, **email is a significant time, money and productivity drain**. We talk with hundreds of busy people every year who are drowning in email. That's not surprising considering the statistics.

According to a report by technology market research firm The Radicati Group, the average corporate email user sends and receives between 105 and 125 email messages per day. Now consider that McKinsey Global Institute and International Data Corp. recently found that managing email is the second most time-consuming activity for workers, devouring about 28 percent of their time. When we take into account that most professionals now handle email from multiple devices, it's easy to see how dealing with email has become such a challenge.

Unfortunately, short of retreating from the work world, there is no silver-bullet solution to the email problem. A first step, however, is to gain clarity on what exactly the problem is. The problem with email is not a technology problem. It is primarily a _human_ problem. The way people handle incoming email and craft outgoing email is often both inefficient and ineffective. Consequently, the solution must be primarily a human solution.

This section covers 10 proven practices for dealing with email – things *you* can do to **make email work for you rather than against you**. Several of these best practices focus on improving your efficiency in handling inbound email. You'll find tips that will show you how to respond promptly to the most important requests and save some serious time managing the rest of your mail.

The remaining best practices focus on improving the effectiveness of your outbound email. In a business world that increasingly relies on email, your ability to drive results is directly connected to your ability to quickly craft clear, succinct, action-oriented emails.

Chances are that your organization is wasting time and money with every email sent and received. These 10 best practices will dramatically reduce the time, cost and stress associated with email. If every person on your team implements the power tools in this section, you will see striking improvements in productivity, communication and morale.

1. Set and Follow Written Standards

As with meeting standards, implementing email standards has a powerful impact on organizational effectiveness, positively affecting both your culture and your bottom line. When everyone within the organization manages their email more efficiently and under the same guidelines, **productivity increases exponentially.**

Standards represent core best practices for how to deal with both inbound and outbound email. Once leadership agrees on basic guidelines, the standards must be communicated organization-wide. They should be posted on the company intranet and constantly reinforced through ongoing training and new employee orientation. Remember, however, that simply setting and communicating standards is not enough. To make an impact, the standards must be lived out every day. When senior leadership not only supports but also *models* the standards, it sends a clear and compelling message to the rest of the organization to get onboard.

One of the most powerful ways to ensure that email standards (and meeting standards for that matter) become engrained in your culture is to recognize and appreciate team members who adopt them. Thank those who model the standards, such as "frontloading" their emails (including all pertinent information early in the message). Remember that what gets *recognized* gets *repeated,* so appreciate that which you want more of. The more you acknowledge those who follow the standards, the more others will take responsibility to follow them, too. When a large percentage of people make it a habit to follow the standards, you will create a culture of efficiency and productivity.

Following are 10 email standards to consider.

Email Standards

1. Keep your inbox clean, current and organized.

2. Answer emails promptly, within one business day (sooner if possible).

3. Know your desired outcomes before you start writing and ensure your email will contribute to achieving your objectives.

4. Include the appropriate people; carefully consider CC and BCC.

5. Clearly state the topic and desired action in the subject line and use the "urgent" indicator sparingly.

6. Be brief, clear and direct and use a courteous, positive, businesslike tone.

7. Stop and think, remembering that what you write is permanent and may become public.

8. Optimize the layout for easy reading.

9. Use a signature block with full contact information on both outgoing messages and replies.

10. Use a personal email account for non-work-related messages.

Inbound

2. Reduce the Volume

The first strategy in managing your inbound mail is to simply reduce the number of emails you receive. This may seem like common sense, but we've found it is not common practice.

According to experts such as Microsoft, **50 percent to 80 percent of incoming email is "graymail."** Unlike spam (unsolicited email that has no real value and is often malicious or illegal), graymail refers to legitimate email from reputable sources that has real content value. Graymail includes requested newsletters and blogs, notifications from sites like LinkedIn, Twitter and Facebook, news updates, and notices from customers and vendors. Much of graymail is initially relevant and may be read on a regular basis. Over time, however, it tends to lose its relevancy or priority, and rather than dealing with it, we allow it to fill up our inbox.

Another culprit fattening up the inbox is old email that hasn't been deleted. A full inbox makes it more difficult to sort and find critical messages. How many times has a crucial email "slipped through the cracks" because it got lost in your inbox? Decluttering your inbox is like cleaning up your desk – it gives you a sense of order.

Eliminating irrelevant emails frees you up to focus on the messages that are most important. Following are tips for reducing the number of incoming emails and decluttering your inbox.

+ **Use a personal email account** for non-work-related messages.

+ **Manage senders.** When copied on emails that you don't want or need, delete them promptly. If the problem persists, talk with team members about your information needs (or lack thereof) or politely ask "repeat offenders" to remove you from their distribution list.

✦ **Unsubscribe** from all except the most content-worthy newsletters and blogs. If you haven't read the last three issues, it isn't relevant. It literally takes less than one minute to unsubscribe (use the link at the bottom of the email). Over the course of a year, that one minute will buy you back hours of productivity.

✦ **Proactively opt out.** When creating online accounts or making online purchases, opt out of any mailing lists. Many websites will automatically add you to their list unless you expressly decline.

✦ **Disable notifications** from social networking sites such as LinkedIn, Twitter and Facebook.

✦ **Say "no" to junk mail.** If you don't want to receive chain letters and jokes, don't send them. Use spam and junk-mail filters in your email application to quarantine junk mail or automatically send it to the trash bin.

✦ **Pick up the phone,** have an ad-hoc, face-to-face conversation or use a messenger application to conduct business that requires quick back-and-forth discussion. You can often resolve in just a few minutes an issue that would take much more time through email.

✦ **Schedule and delete.** For emails that relate to your calendar (such as meetings), schedule the event on your calendar immediately. Insert pertinent information, attachments (e.g., the agenda or pre-reading) or the email itself into the calendar event and then delete the original from your inbox.

✦ **Don't be afraid to delete!** If you miss something important, someone will remind you. Delete emails that relate to actions you've performed or obligations you've fulfilled when no other important information is contained in the message. Delete all previous emails in a conversation, especially if the entire thread is included in the latest version. Delete email with large attachments that you've saved elsewhere on your computer.

Inbound

3. Create a System that Works for You

In today's connected world, we are "live" all of the time. Most of us receive and manage email on various devices – tablets, laptops, desktop computers and possibly even multiple phones. To complicate matters even more, many people have several email accounts. The old "rules" for effectively managing incoming email may not be the best solutions in an always-on, tech-savvy world.

Today, there is no one-size-fits-all solution. **You have to create a system for sorting and handling incoming email that works for *you*** – your schedule, your devices, your work style, your company's protocols. Figure out which email activities and processes maximize your effectiveness and make them your personal best practices.

Consider talking with your colleagues about how they manage their email. Find out what works well for them. We often don't think to ask our co-workers about their best practices, yet they are typically excellent resources because they work in a similar environment and within the same parameters as we do. A 5- to 10-minute conversation with a few colleagues can yield a wealth of tips and ideas.

In addition to seeking best practices within your own organization, here are basic tips for handling incoming email, which apply to almost any scenario:

✦ **Leverage resources.** If you have an assistant, work together to identify ways s/he can help handle your email. Many busy executives and professionals fail to maximize resources by not having their assistants sort, organize, reroute and even answer some (if not the majority) of incoming email.

✦ **Organize with descriptive folders.** Use folders to categorize and file your emails. The more descriptive the folder names, the easier it will be to manage, respond to and search for email. Emails can also be categorized by month, project, employee, topic, customer, etc. For a more detailed system, use folders and subfolders. For example: a folder titled *Customers* with subfolders for each major customer.

✦ **Use automatic filing filters or rules.** Many email applications have sophisticated filtering systems that will automatically delete, flag, move or file email based on specific criteria. Using these automatic filters in conjunction with descriptive folders makes for a very efficient system.

✦ **Save time by saving.** Some emails don't need to be read right away but rather saved for future reference, for example, status reports on ongoing projects, sales or financial reports, etc. Use simple criteria to organize and save these emails in descriptive folders so you can easily find them if the need arises.

✦ **Start, even if you can't finish.** People often don't think about the strategy of doing something partially. Sometimes, the best way to tackle an important email is to start it while ideas are fresh in your mind, file it in your "Drafts" folder and think on it for a bit, and then finish it at a later time. This technique works well when you don't readily have all of the facts or information needed to complete an email. It's also an effective way to leverage your time – if you have 5 minutes at the airport, you can at least get started on an email.

✦ **Customize.** Ask your team and those you exchange email with regularly to send you email the way you want to receive it, for example, always copying your assistant or putting the "ask" in the subject line.

Inbound/Outbound

4. Determine What You Want to Accomplish

Having a clear idea about what you want to accomplish provides the foundation for effective emails that drive the best results. First, consider whether email is even the best method for communicating your message. Most people communicate in their most comfortable mode (for many of us, that is email), whether it's the best fit for the message or not. Some topics, such as sensitive matters or emotional subjects, are better handled in person or by phone.

If you determine that an email is the best communication method for your message, take a brief moment to think about your desired outcome. Quickly run through the Reporter's Questions:

What	What is the general purpose of the email (e.g., request action, gather information, create a dialogue, share information)?
Who	Who should the email be sent to (who needs to take action) and who, if anyone, should be copied (who just needs the information)?
When	When does an email need to be sent?
Why	What's in it for others to help me accomplish the objective?
How	How can I best communicate my message? What information do I need to include?

Once you've identified your objectives, utilize the type of email that will best help you achieve that objective:

✦ **Action Emails** – The goal is to move the recipient to take action, for example, a sales pitch in which you're asking for the sale. The *action* is your desired outcome. The clearer you are about what you want, the better you can tailor the email for the intended result and the more likely you will be to achieve your desired outcome. Use action emails to:

◆ Deliver action plans or priority lists;

◆ Schedule meetings or phone calls;

◆ Assign responsibilities.

✦ **Inquiry Emails** – The goal is to gain information. The *reply* is your desired outcome. Use inquiry emails to:

◆ Ask questions;

◆ Invite advice or feedback;

◆ Request information;

◆ Inquire on the status of action plans, projects, reports, etc.;

◆ Seek clarification.

✦ **Dialogue Emails** – The goal is to establish communication with the recipient for some future result or benefit, for example, a potential strategic alliance. Your desired outcome is to *create a connection*. Use dialogue emails to:

◆ Initiate or continue a relationship;

◆ Share information, insights and perspective.

✦ **Self-Fulfilling Emails** – The goal is to share information with the recipient, with no reply necessary. The *content* itself is the desired outcome. You want to tell the receiver something, such as give them a compliment. Use self-fulfilling emails to:

◆ Recognize performance;

◆ Share thoughts and information;

◆ Show appreciation or gratitude.

 **Inbound/Outbound**

5. Frontload Your Emails with Action

Frontloading your emails with action guarantees that recipients get the most vital information as soon as possible. It also ensures that your key message is communicated even if the reader doesn't finish the email. The primary ways to frontload your emails are: 1) to fully leverage the subject line, and 2) to state the purpose of the email in the opening. Let's look at each of these best practices.

Leverage the Subject Line
Use the subject line of every email to quickly and clearly communicate what you want to accomplish. **The subject line should tell the reader at a glance the topic, question or desired action and help the reader prioritize the email.** Ideally, the recipient shouldn't have to open the email to know what it is about. Consider the compelling differences between the vague subject lines below and their crystal-clear, action-oriented counterparts:

Poor Subject Lines	Powerful Subject Lines
Meeting	Staff meeting July 23 @ 9 am – confirmation needed
Please call me	Call me re: Andy Smith resume
Per your request	Attaching meeting notes per your request
When you get a minute	I need your help today on …
Question	Question: Where is the agenda?
Project	Before the 22nd, I need your help on …

Here are a few more tips for leveraging the subject line:

✦ Never leave the subject empty.

✦ Be sure to update the subject in a reply or forward if the topic has changed.

✦ Give as much detail as space allows.

✦ Abbreviate and use symbols when possible.

✦ Use words such as "hot" or "urgent" only when special attention is truly warranted.

✦ Ask for a response by a specified date or time only when you're on a tight timetable.

State Your Purpose Quickly and Clearly

When it comes to the body of the email, choose the first few words carefully and get to the point immediately. **Your "ask" or "tell" should appear in the first sentence.** People are more likely to do what you ask if they don't have to wade through the rest of the email to determine how best to respond.

✦ State your point or purpose clearly, using minimal words.

✦ If action is needed, make it clear what you need from the recipient, for example, "Please answer three questions."

✦ When multiple recipients are involved, provide a clear call to action for each person.

✦ If no action or reply is expected, say "No reply necessary."

✦ When emailing someone for the first time, open by introducing yourself (giving context if necessary) and explain why you are emailing them.

Inbound/Outbound ▬▬▬▬▬▬▬▬

6. Optimize the Content and Layout

The specific content you include in an email – and how that content is presented – can make a significant difference in how well your email is received and how quickly it is acted upon. Choosing which content to include is a balancing act. **You want to give just enough information so that people can respond intelligently and without coming back to you for clarification.**

As you begin writing your email, give some thought as to what information needs to be included. What does the recipient need to know (that they don't know already) in order to take action or answer your question? Here are great tips for choosing your email content:

✦ Know your audience and adjust the level of detail accordingly.

✦ Anticipate recipients' questions to help you determine what information needs to be included.

✦ Utilize pictures and graphics if the information is relevant.

✦ For long or complicated content, draft the message in your word processor first, and then copy and paste it into an email. Note that some complex content is best covered in person or by phone.

✦ Attach any relevant documents.

✦ If emailing to schedule a meeting, outline the agenda or include it as an attachment.

✦ Delete non-related or out-of-date prior messages in the email string or reference important ones (e.g., "See Pat's note two down in this string").

✦ Include a hyperlink if referencing a website.

Layout is a key factor in email effectiveness. Your carefully selected content will lose its impact if it is not formatted in such a way that the reader can easily digest it. Below are guidelines for content layout:

✦ Make it legible – choose a font style, size (at least 11 pt.) and color that are readable and not distracting.

✦ Avoid script fonts and light colors. Don't use colored or patterned backgrounds.

✦ Include background information in the body of the email rather than in the opening.

✦ Write in short, separated paragraphs with subheadings as necessary.

✦ Use bullet points and numbered lists instead of lengthy paragraphs.

✦ Number questions for easier and clearer responses.

✦ Sort action items, questions and requests by name when multiple recipients are involved, and use a bold font for each name.

✦ Highlight or use bold font to add emphasis to keywords, phrases and information.

✦ Organize information and data in tables, charts or graphs.

✦ Use a signature block on all outbound emails – those you initiate as well as replies and forwards – including your full name, title, phone number(s) and email address.

Inbound/Outbound ▬▬▬▬▬▬▬▬

7. Make It Easy

As evidenced by the statistics we shared at the beginning of this section, people are drowning in email. If you can communicate in a way that creates more clarity and leads to fewer questions, you will reduce the amount of back-and-forth needed to accomplish your objective(s). **Anything you can do to make it easier for recipients to respond quickly and completely to your email creates a win/win.**

✦ **Be brief.**
Brevity is essential if you want your email to be read. The longer the email, the more likely your recipient will wait to respond until he/she has more time. Limit emails to one screen and a single subject whenever possible. **Try emailing like you text** – when you use mobile devices, you get to the point quickly and use as few words as possible.

✦ **Be clear.**
Taking into account what we just said about being brief, clarity trumps brevity. **Brief is good, but brief, clear, concise and action-oriented is better.** If you need an extra sentence to ensure clarity, put it in. Use simple language (again, think about texting), and if you must use acronyms, be sure to explain them.

✦ **Be sensitive to handheld users.**
With so many people processing email on handheld devices, it is wise to take that into consideration. For example, sometimes it's best to include information in the body of the email rather than as an attachment (or do both). Instead of sending large attachments, upload files to a web-based file-sharing service.

✦ Minimize questions and action items.
Limit the number of questions you ask or action items you assign to four or fewer. The more questions (especially open-ended questions) asked in one email, the less likely you are to get a response. Likewise, the more action items you assign, the less likely you are to get results.

✦ Provide a complete response.
When responding to an email, read it carefully and be sure you address all of the sender's items or questions. It is more informative – and reduces time-wasting back-and-forth emails – to say, "I don't know about..." than to simply ignore an item or question.

✦ Think about "To" versus "CC."
Earlier in this section, we suggested that when identifying your objective(s) for an email, you consider who needs to take action on the email versus who simply needs the information. This distinction is important because it determines who the email is actually sent to (those who need to take action) and who gets copied (those who need information only). Distinguishing between "To" and "CC" is a way of signaling to recipients who is expected to respond or act and who is not.

✦ Proofread and edit.
Always proofread emails before sending. As time permits, edit to trim words, sentences and details that do not add to the main point. Clear up any potential ambiguities. Check for and remove excess commentary that doesn't contribute to your desired result.

Inbound/Outbound

8. Get It "Good Enough" and Get It Out

One of the keys to productivity in our do-more-with-less, need-it-yesterday world is to complete tasks and projects in reduced timeframes. Speed is admired and sought after in today's business environment. Obviously, if you can produce more work in less time, you will see results much faster.

Of all the things you can control with respect to your production, perfectionism and procrastination have the biggest negative impact on speed and, therefore, results. Many people fail to act quickly because their self-talk says, "I have to make it perfect." Nothing prohibits achievement more than procrastination, and the idea that everything has to be just right or perfect before one can begin is the foundational concept that supports procrastination.

In school, we often learned the hard way that an "A" paper turned in late was not as good as a "B+" paper turned in before the deadline. The same holds true in business – in most cases, something done **90 percent right and fast beats 100 percent right and too late.**

The concept of *Production Before Perfection* (PBP) is the solution to perfection-related procrastination and a catalyst for great results. The concept is simple: You don't have to have all of the answers before you can start working! *Production Before Perfection* flies in the face of waiting and demands action now. In other words, act first and get it perfect later!

This principle holds true in many work-related situations, but particularly so with email. In most cases, **the value of a perfect**

email is far outweighed by the benefits gained from getting that email out quickly. Of course, your emails need to be accurate and professional, but they don't have to be perfect. With as many emails as you must process, perfection is an unattainable goal anyway. More to the point, when you hold yourself to an extreme standard, the most likely effect is to cripple your ability to act.

Production Before Perfection applies to virtually all emails but is especially true for emails that have explicit or implicit time value. Consider this scenario: It's 4:30 p.m. and you've just learned of a problem in your area that is going to be shared with management in a meeting tomorrow morning. You need to alert your boss. Don't wait until you have all of the information. Send an email *now* with as much information as you have and follow up later by phone with an update.

Here is another example: You receive new data that will materially affect a meeting you've called for tomorrow. Rather than spending an hour getting the data formatted "just right," get it out quickly to the people who are coming to your meeting.

Effective email is not about perfection, it's about achieving your objectives. Let go of any inclination you might have to achieve perfection – especially with email. Don't waste valuable time by chasing diminishing results. Live by the maxim, **"How good is good enough?"**

When it comes to email, seek *Production Before Perfection* – get it "good enough" and get it out!

Inbound/Outbound

9. Give Respect, Get Results

Oftentimes, as the originator of an email, you are asking people to help you accomplish your objective, either by providing you with information, answering a question or taking action. Being respectful and courteous when asking for someone's help is just common sense. As we mentioned with respect to meetings, even if you can require people to act on your emails because you're the boss, you'll achieve better results faster if you show others respect.

While email is a great communication tool, it tends to desensitize us to people's needs, emotions, reactions and realities. What we don't see, we often forget. That is why **it's important when communicating via email to intentionally show respect for others' priorities, efforts and time.**

Respect Others' Priorities

Whether you are the boss, a colleague, or a team member, you need to recognize that people you interact with have other things going on. Just because you have an issue that needs to be dealt with promptly doesn't mean that others will receive it with the same degree of urgency or level of priority.

Respect people's priorities by taking into account their other work and realistically assigning deadlines and timelines. Overusing the email "high priority" indicator and the phrase "need today" or "urgent" will make your team immune to the truly important matters. Avoid the "Chicken Little – the sky is falling" alert if the issue isn't both important and urgent. On those rare occasions when you do urgently need support, be sure to indicate that in your subject line, for example, "I need your help **today** on …."

Furthermore, using descriptors such as "hot," "top priority" and "urgent" will likely leave your recipients – and you – frustrated because these terms are open to interpretation. "Urgent" might mean *today* to you but *this week* to someone on your team. Respect others' priorities and time by being very specific in your requests, for example, "Before the 22nd, I need your help on...."

Respect Others' Efforts

Have you ever worked diligently on a project, proposal or report, sent it off via email to someone and then...nothing? You never receive a response. You wonder...was it lost in cyberspace? Did they receive it but aren't satisfied with the work? Or, is everything fine, and they simply haven't responded? Wouldn't it be nice to know?

When someone sends you work via email, take a brief moment to acknowledge that you received it (even if you haven't reviewed it yet). A simple response not only allows the sender to relax, but also shows respect for the time and effort required to produce the work. We suggest a brief addition to the subject line that lets the receiver know at a glance that their email was received. For example:

Original subject line – January Inventory Report

Response – Re: January Inventory Report – Rec'd, thanks!

Remember, too, that gratitude is always appreciated. Close emails with a brief but sincere thank you, such as "Thanks for your help on this important item."

Respect Others' Time

When you send out a long, tedious email, you are essentially saying, "I don't respect your time." Show people you appreciate their time by keeping emails short, clear and simple to answer. Another way to respect others' time is to avoid "Reply All" unless everyone really does need to receive your reply. And finally, get emails out as soon as inquiries or requests are identified. Don't put others in a time crunch because you didn't promptly send out an email.

Inbound/Outbound

10. Think Before You Hit "Send"

Earlier, we talked about *Production Before Perfection* and the value of getting emails out in a timely manner even if they're not flawless. While you don't want to procrastinate in sending out an email, you do want to take a brief moment before you hit "Send" to think about what you are communicating. **Email is like any other communication – it either adds to or subtracts from your personal reputation and your corporate brand.**

What you write in an email is permanent and may become public. Yet because email is so quick and easy to use, it tends to encourage reactive, off-the-cuff responses that can be problematic. As we've all seen repeatedly in the media, careers can be ruined by just one inappropriate or incorrectly sent email. Here are some areas to consider before you send that next email:

Check the Tone

In person, communication is approximately 55 percent body language, 38 percent tonality and only 7 percent actual words used. With email, the largest portion of communication – body language – is completely removed. As a result, the words you use and especially your tone play a major role in how your message is received. And because the non-verbal cues are missing, tone and context are easy to misread or misinterpret.

When using email, the safest bet is to **always assume that if your message can be misunderstood, it will be.** In every email, thoughtfully consider how your words and tone may be perceived and always do a quick "tone check" before you hit "Send":

✦ Interject your personality into your emails, but don't try to be funny – the chances of being misunderstood are simply too great.

✦ Avoid sarcasm – it almost always offends someone.

✦ Keep it clean – refrain from sending gossip or inappropriate emails to anyone's business email.

Manage Your Emotions

Even in the most civilized organizations, emotions can sometimes get the best of us. Face-to-face contact or a phone conversation is always the best option for emotionally charged topics. If distance or schedules make phone or in-person contacts impractical and you must use email, don't send it right away. Give yourself some time to process the situation and calm down. This is one of the few times when it is better to wait before sending an email. Emails sent "in the heat of the moment" tend to escalate problems rather than solve them.

Draft the email very carefully avoiding "hot" words, ALL CAPS (shouting), threats, criticisms and highly judgmental statements. Move the email to your drafts folder and let it cool for a few hours or preferably overnight. Then review it and make adjustments. Once your emotions have settled, you will likely see the benefit of changing the wording and tone of an email to help de-escalate the situation. (You may also want to ask a trusted co-worker to give it a "tone check.") If you are still convinced the email needs to go and is appropriate, press the Send button.

Use CC and BCC Carefully

Both CC and BCC are great tools, but both are overused. Carefully consider who should be copied or blind copied. If receivers might use "Reply All," what are the potential implications of all recipients seeing everyone's responses? Avoid blind copies, as they can be controversial if exposed.

Email VIPs
(Very Important Points)

1. Set and follow written standards. Email standards represent core best practices for how to deal with both inbound and outbound email. When everyone within the organization manages their email more efficiently and under the same guidelines, productivity increases exponentially and expectations are consistently met.

INBOUND

2. Reduce the volume. Eliminate graymail – legitimate email from reputable sources that has lost its relevancy. De-clutter your inbox by deleting old emails and setting up filters so you can focus on the messages that are most important.

3. Create a system that works for you. There is no one-size-fits-all solution for handling email. Create a system that maximizes your effectiveness and works with your schedule, your devices, your work style, and your company's protocols.

OUTBOUND

4. Determine what you want to accomplish. Having clarity about your objective(s) provides the foundation for effective emails. Consider the *what, who, when, why* and *how* before you start writing. Then, utilize the type of email – action, inquiry, dialog or self-fulfilling – that will drive the best results.

5. Front-load your emails with action. Front-loading your emails with action guarantees that recipients get the most vital information as soon as possible. Leverage the subject line by clearly describing the specific topic, question or desired action. Then, get to the point immediately by including your "ask" or "tell" in the first sentence.

6. **Optimize the content and layout.** Give enough information for people to respond without coming back for clarification, but no more. Then lay out your content clearly so that the reader can easily digest it.

7. **Make it easy.** Anything you can do to make it easier for recipients to respond quickly and completely to your email creates a win/win. Try emailing like you text – be brief, clear and to the point. Consider how emails appear to handheld users. Keep questions and action items to four or fewer. Use a signature block with full contact information on both outgoing messages and replies.

8. **Get it "good enough" and get it out.** Effective email is not about perfection, it's about achieving your objectives. Seek *Production Before Perfection* – 90 percent right and fast beats 100 percent right and too late. Live by the maxim, "How good is good enough?"

9. **Give respect, get results.** When communicating via email, intentionally respect others' priorities, efforts and time. Avoid overusing the "high priority" indicator and the phrase "need today." When someone sends you work via email, take a moment to acknowledge that you received it if you can't answer and close it out immediately.

10. **Think before you hit "Send."** Email either adds to or subtracts from your personal reputation and your corporate brand. Tone and context are easy to misread or misinterpret. Always assume that if your message can be misunderstood, it will be. Emotionally charged topics are best handled by phone or in-person, but if you must use email, don't send it right away.

Sample Emails

Example #1

Ineffective Email

From: John
Date: Wednesday, October 21
To: Aaron; Web Update Team
Cc: Sarah
Subject: RE: Blog Post

> Because the Web Update Team needs this information but does not need to take action, they should be copied on the email rather than included in the "To" section.

> If Sarah, John's boss, does not need this level of detailed information, she should not be copied on the email.

> The topic of the email has changed from blog post to website revisions but the title does not reflect that change.

Hi Aaron,

Wanted to check on the website upgrade. I sent a new image for the home page. Were you able to use it? I also sent you a new mock-up and a request to change the text on the Contact Us page. Did you get those and did they make sense? When do you think these items will be completed?

Thanks!

John

> The content is not concise, and the format and layout are not helpful to the reader.

IT Project Manager
(123) 456-7890
John.Doe@ABCcompany.com

From: John
Date: Monday, October 12
To: Aaron
Subject: Blog Post

> Unrelated included message in the email string.

Aaron –

Attached is this week's blog post to be uploaded to the website. Please confirm receipt. Thanks.

Effective, Powerful and Results-Oriented Email:

From: John
Date: Wednesday, October 21
To: Aaron
Cc: Web Update Team
Subject: Status of Website Revisions

> Web Update Team is appropriately copied on the email since no action is required by them. John's boss Sarah does not get unnecessary email in her inbox.

> Subject line clearly communicates the topic at a glance.

Hi Aaron,

> The "ask" is frontloaded in the first sentence, and the action needed is clear.

Can you please give me the status of the following items relating to our website update as well as your best estimate of when these items will be completed:

1. Were you able to use the new image for the home page?

2. Did you see my latest request to change the text on the Contact Us page?

3. Did the new mock-up I sent you make sense?

> Questions are numbered for easier reading and response.

Thanks!

John Doe

IT Project Manager
(123) 456-7890
John.Doe@ABCcompany.com

> Previous, unrelated messages have been removed from the email string.

Sample Emails
Example #2

Ineffective Email

From: Chris
Date: Thursday, May 10
To: Kim, Jesse, Mark, Lisa, Alex
Subject: Proposal

> Subject line is vague and not action oriented.

Hi Team,

> Script font is difficult to read, especially in a light color, and too informal for business use.

We need to get the proposal for XYZ Company out ASAP. In order to do that, we need to price out the project, develop the scope and sequence of work, gather the applicable information from the training department and confirm subcontractor availability. And then, of course, we need to compile all of these components into a final document.

Please keep me updated on the status of these and let me know how I can help. Thanks!

Chris

> Contact information is missing.

> Message is unclear regarding who is responsible for what action items.

Effective, Powerful and Results-Oriented Email:

From: Chris
Date: Thursday, May 10
To: Kim, Jesse, Mark, Lisa, Alex
Subject: XYZ Proposal – Action Needed by Tuesday, May 15th

> Subject line clearly communicates topic and timing at a glance.

Team –

> Action is front-loaded. Actions are sorted by the person who is responsible for each, and that person's name is highlighted with bold font. Actions are bulleted for easier reading.

Below are actions needed to complete the proposal for XYZ Company. Each piece should be forwarded to Alex no later than end of day on Tuesday, May 15th so he can compile the proposal and forward to me for review.

- **Kim:** price out the project

- **Jesse:** develop the scope and sequence of work

- **Mark:** gather the applicable information from the training department

- **Lisa:** confirm subcontractor availability

- **Alex:** compile all of these components into a final document and forward to me no later than end of day Thursday, May 17th

Please confirm receipt of this email and keep me updated on the status of your respective pieces. I'm available to assist if you have questions or need help. Thanks!

Chris Smith
Account Manager
(123) 456-7890
Jane.Doe@ABCcompany.com

> Font is more legible.

> Signature block contains full contact information.

Getting Started

The benefits of improving your meeting management and email practices are clearly worth the effort to bring about change. Implementation of the best practices in this book pay back very rapidly based on time savings alone. The larger paybacks, in terms of communications effectiveness and results, will come quickly as well. You can transform the communication culture of your organization by adopting the best practices in this book, training your team to execute them and then reinforcing their efforts until the practices become corporate habits.

The change to more effective and efficient meetings and emails starts with you. You are the catalyst that can get the ball rolling. Getting started involves establishing your own commitment to managing meetings and handling emails differently and then gathering enough support to reach critical mass. People spend so much wasted time in unproductive meetings and dealing with email that they are ready for positive change. You simply have to spread the word and offer resources and support.

1. **Spread the word** with a compelling, "back of the envelope" presentation that shares your belief in a strong case for change in your organization:

   ✦ We all spend a tremendous amount of time in meetings and reading and writing emails. Even modest steps to cut wasted time will save money and improve results.

   ✦ The potential results more than justify taking immediate action. Exceptional meetings and efficient handling of email can make a significant positive impact on the quality of each team member's professional life.

✦ "It's not brain surgery" – The best practices that can drive change are common sense and can easily be implemented in just a few hours. Some may take some getting used to and refinement to put into habits but will be worth the effort in results achieved.

2. **Offer the support** that will drive real transformation in your organization. Get people the resources they need to redefine the work of managing meetings and handling emails, which most people dread, to *High Leverage Activities* (HLAs) that will consistently deliver high-quality results. Investing in the right resources will produce a huge Return on Investment (ROI) and Return on Effort (ROE):

✦ Get this book in the hands of all of your colleagues, whether your team has 5, 50, 500 or 5,000 people.

✦ If you have 500 employees or more in your organization, you can literally change your communication culture in two hours by training everyone on your team on these best practices.

Get started now! Select a starting point, establish your own commitment to the work, and determine how to gather enough support to reach critical mass. If you're at the top of the house, don't be afraid to be forceful in your recommendations. Increased productivity, enhanced morale and better results are waiting. Take action today!

About the Authors

George Lowe is an independent consultant working with clients in a variety of industries on communications, presentations, meetings, event management and organizational development matters. Earlier, he worked in the automotive industry for over 30 years in a wide variety of leadership roles with Ford Motor Company in Quality, Service, Sales, Marketing, and Product Development, both in the U.S. and globally. Later, he joined one of his clients as VP Operations, returning to consulting at the conclusion of that assignment.

Core to his consulting practice is a relentless drive for clarity in both thinking and communications, while closely focusing on customer requirements. He holds a Bachelor's Degree from Western Michigan University (Cum Laude) and an MBA from Michigan State University. He can be contacted at georgelowe@ameritech.net.

Tony Jeary – is a thought leader, prolific author and keynote speaker. He coaches and advises many of the world's top CEOs, including the presidents of Ford, TGI Fridays, Texaco, American Airlines, Walmart, Firestone, Samsung and New York Life. Tony teaches clients how to transform Visions into Reality in Compressed Time, leveraging the methodology of CLARITY, FOCUS and EXECUTION from his best-selling book *Strategic Acceleration*.

Tony and his team impact results. He continually practices his business mantra, "Give Value...Do More Than Is Expected." Tony works with special clients from his private studio on his estate in the DFW area. The unique and inspiring environment he's created contains decades of organized best practices that facilitate executive team "experiences" unlike any other. Tony can be booked through www.tonyjeary.com.

☑ YES! Please send me extra copies of *We've Got to Start Meeting & Emailing Like This!*

1-30 copies $14.95   31-100 copies $13.95   100+ copies $12.95

We've Got to Start Meeting &
  Emailing Like This!   ____ copies X _____   = $ _____

Additional Leadership Development Resources

136 Effective Presentation Tips	____ copies X $ 9.95	= $ _____
Monday Morning Leadership	____ copies X $14.95	= $ _____
TIME!	____ copies X $12.95	= $ _____
The Eight Constants of Change	____ copies X $14.95	= $ _____

Shipping & Handling $ _____

Subtotal $ _____

Sales Tax (8.25%-TX Only) $ _____

Total (U.S. Dollars Only) $ _____

Shipping and Handling Charges

Total $ Amount	Up to $49	$50-$99	$100-$249	$250-$1199	$1200-$2999	$3000+
Charge	$7	$9	$16	$30	$80	$125

Name _____ Job Title _____

Organization _____ Phone _____

Shipping Address _____ Fax _____

Billing Address _____ Email _____
                                              (Required for downloadable products)

City _____ State _____ ZIP _____

❑ Please invoice (Orders over $200) Purchase Order Number (if applicable) _____

Charge Your Order: ❑ MasterCard   ❑ Visa   ❑ American Express

Credit Card Number _____ Exp. Date _____

Signature _____

❑ Check Enclosed (Payable to: CornerStone Leadership)

Fax	**Mail**	**Phone**
972.274.2884	**P.O. Box 764087**	**972.298.8377**
	Dallas, TX 75376	

Thank you for reading
We've Got to Start Meeting & Emailing Like This!

We hope it has assisted you in your quest for personal and professional growth. CornerStone Leadership is committed to providing new and enlightening products to organizations worldwide.

Our mission is to fuel knowledge with practical resources that will accelerate your team's productivity, success and job satisfaction!

Best wishes for your continued success.

CornerStone
Leadership Institute

*Start a crusade in your organization –
have the courage to learn, the vision to lead,
and the passion to share.*